World Religions

Judaism: *The People of the Promise*

Passover

At Pesach (Passover) Jewish families gather for Seder, a joyful meal that celebrates in food, song and ritual God's rescue of the Israelites from Egypt. One dish includes five special foods each with symbolic meaning – an egg, green vegetables dipped in salty water, lamb shankbone, bitter herbs, usually horseradish, and a sweet paste eaten with matzah, unleavened bread, because the people fled Egypt in such a hurry their bread did not have time to rise.

'Hear O Israel, the Lord our God, the Lord is one.'

THE SHEMA, A PRAYER SAID DAILY

JEWS BELIEVE THAT for some 4,000 years there has been a unique relationship between God and the Jewish people. During this history the memory of journeys of exile and return has deeply influenced Judaism.

In the first journey, around 1800 BC, the Bible records that Abraham answered God's call to travel to Mesopotamia to a new land where God would make a great nation out of his descendants. Abraham travelled to Canaan, part of what is Israel and Palestine today. Jewish tradition interprets Abraham's journey as the rejection of idolatry and the acceptance of monotheism, that is, belief in one God whose presence is everywhere.

The second journey was a journey of escape from slavery. Abraham's descendants moved to Egypt where they were enslaved, until, led by Moses around 1200 BC, they fled across the Red Sea to freedom. Jewish scripture recalls how God struck the Egyptians with ten plagues to make them let the Israelites go.

The final plague of death of the first-born 'passed over' the Israelites, leaving them unscathed. This rescue reinforced the Jewish sense of distinctiveness, and Jews celebrate these events each year at Passover. The liberated Hebrew people then gathered at Mount Sinai where their relationship with God was solemnised, binding all Jews to the Law, or Torah, which God gave them there.

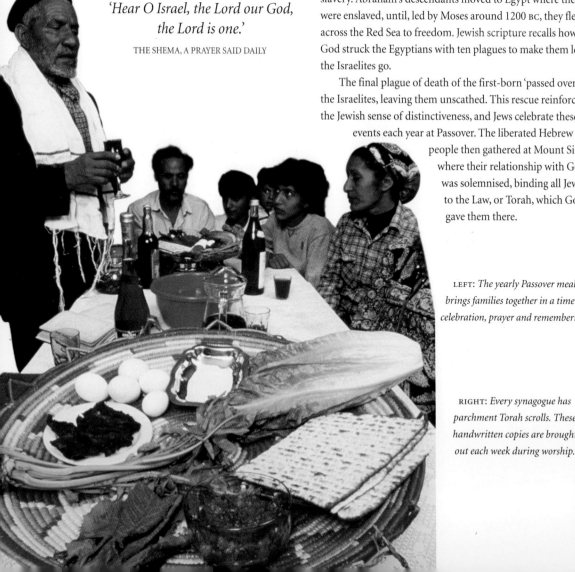

LEFT: *The yearly Passover meal brings families together in a time of celebration, prayer and remembering*

RIGHT: *Every synagogue has parchment Torah scrolls. These handwritten copies are brought out each week during worship.*

After reconquering Canaan, a kingship evolved, with King David an outstanding leader. His son Solomon built the Temple in Jerusalem, which became the centre of Jewish worship until the people were carried into exile in Babylon and their temple destroyed. This exile is often seen as the consequence of the people's lapsing into sin and turning away from God. They were subsequently set free by the Persian King Cyrus, and this freedom, with the rebuilding of the Temple and Jewish life, is viewed as repentance and return.

After the destruction of the Temple by the Romans in AD 70 Jewish worship centred on synagogues, on intensive study of scripture, and on prayer and ritual in the home. Rabbis replaced the hereditary caste of priests. Judaism began increasingly to look towards the coming of a Messiah, a descendant of David, who would usher in a new age of peace and justice.

Sent into exile once again by the Romans, Jewish communities spread throughout the world. Discrimination and persecution, such as their expulsion from Spain in 1492, culminated in the Holocaust, when the Nazis decimated the Jewish population of Europe in 1939–45.

The birth of the state of Israel in 1948 is often seen as a new experience of return from exile, the gathering in of God's people from their exile in different lands. This experience of renewal is sometimes interpreted as the beginning of redemption or the Messianic era.

...Jewish Faith and Life

God's call to the Hebrew people promised his blessing on them, but also challenged them to live his laws as an example to others. This relationship between God and the people is called the covenant. Every Jewish male carries the mark of the covenant on his body, because according to scripture God told Abraham that each male should be circumcised as a sign of the covenant. The importance of the covenant was emphasised during awesome events which the Bible records at Mount Sinai, where Moses conveyed to the people God's renewed summons to a special relationship.

This history is preserved in the first five books of the Jewish Bible: Genesis, Exodus, Leviticus, Numbers and Deuteronomy. They include accounts of the creation, the history of the patriarchs, and detailed ritual and cultural laws. The rest of the Bible contains the Prophets, and Writings (such as the Psalms). The first five books are sometimes attributed to Moses and called Torah, but Torah can also mean teaching, law, or instruction, and is sometimes extended to mean all sacred and legal texts down to the Middle Ages, including oral law.

In a strictly Jewish home, faith and ritual pervade everyday activities. Jewish tradition counts 613 *mitzvot*, or commandments. They range from the high ethical principles of the Ten Commandments to details about dietary laws, such as the separation of meat and dairy products. Among the commandments is the keeping of the Sabbath, a 24-hour period beginning on a Friday evening, free from work and distraction, set aside for the renewal of faith and family life.

ABOVE: *At his bar mitzvah a Jewish boy marks his coming of age by reading a portion of the Torah. This bar mitzvah is taking place at the Western Wall in Jerusalem, Israel.*

Some Jews believe that God dictated the whole Torah (i.e. the first five books of the Jewish Bible) to Moses at Sinai. Others, following modern scholarship, believe that it was composed by many hands over many years. In the mid-19th century a new movement, Reform Judaism, began in Germany and moved away from Orthodox Judaism. Reform Judaism sought to reconcile Judaism with western scholarship and a more modern world view. It is more relaxed towards the commandments about food, dress and ritual, and has modernised its synagogue services. It grants full equality to women in the synagogue and has female clergy.

Synagogues face towards Jerusalem and, because of the commandment against idolatry, they contain no sculpture. Against the eastern wall is the Holy Ark, a cupboard, often beautifully ornate, which contains the Torah on hand-written parchment scrolls. A light burns in front of it as a reminder of God's spiritual presence. The service is conducted from a dais and consists of readings from scripture, prayers and songs of praise. During services the Sefer Torah, or scroll, is carried in procession around the synagogue. There are special services for high holy days such as Yom Kippur (Day of Atonement), Rosh Hashanah (New Year), and the old pilgrim festivals of Passover, Pentecost and Tabernacles.

BELOW: *At the Hanukkah festival the lighting of the menorah candlestick commemorates the recapturing of the Temple in the 2nd century BC from those who had turned it into a Greek pagan temple. Each night over eight days the family gathers to light the menorah, reciting special blessings.*

ABOVE: *A service at a Liberal synagogue in Tel Aviv, Israel. In Liberal synagogues women and men sit together, rather than separately as in other synagogues.*

LEFT: *Hasidic Jews in their distinctive dress. The Hasidic movement arose in Eastern Europe in the 18th century. It is based on traditional mysticism and seeks to bring the soul closer to God through ecstatic worship that uses song, praise and even dance.*

Christianity: The Life of the Founder

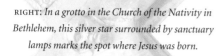

RIGHT: *In a grotto in the Church of the Nativity in Bethlehem, this silver star surrounded by sanctuary lamps marks the spot where Jesus was born.*

BELOW: *Many churches mark Christmas by building a crib or Nativity scene, recalling the stable in Bethlehem, now in Israel, where Jesus was born.*

CHRISTIANITY, AS ITS NAME IMPLIES, is inspired by the life and teachings of Jesus Christ. Christ is not a name: it is a title, or description. It means 'the Anointed One', and is the translation of the Hebrew Messiah. Christians believe that the Church continues the sacred history begun in the story of the Jews. Hence Christians also revere the Jewish Bible and name it the Old Testament, while the Christian story is in the New Testament.

For centuries before the birth of Jesus the Jewish people awaited a saviour, or Messiah, to rescue God's people from suffering. Our main sources for the life of Jesus are the Gospels. As they look back they see Jesus fulfilling those hopes for a divine break-through. This divine initiative is signalled by the way his mother, Mary, remains a virgin, and conceives Jesus by the power of the Holy Spirit.

When Jesus was about 30 he began an itinerant ministry of preaching and healing, accompanied by a band of disciples. His message had two aspects in particular. He asked his hearers to accept that the Kingdom of God was at hand. Flowing from this was his call to repent, to begin a new way of life based on compassion, forgiveness and generosity. He illustrated his preaching with parables, stories based on the things of everyday life such as seeds, journeys, weddings, a wastrel son, a lost coin. However, these stories usually have a challenging twist at the end.

Much of the teaching and preaching of Jesus took place around the Sea of Galilee.

Many of the parables describe the Kingdom of God as a new era in which human conduct increasingly reflects God's love. The friendship of Jesus was often extended to outcasts, to symbolise the inclusiveness of this Kingdom. Against this has to be balanced another side of Jesus, in which he speaks of God's judgement which will separate the good and the wicked. His healing miracles were taken to be a sign of divine power.

The growing popularity of Jesus alarmed civic and religious leaders, especially when he moved to Jerusalem. The authorities ordered his execution by crucifixion. To his followers his death on the Cross seemed the end of all their hopes, until the news came that his tomb was empty. This was a sign that he was not among the dead but among the living, a sign confirmed, according to the New Testament, by several appearances in which Jesus moved among his people and spoke to them. The power of God had overcome death. The followers of Jesus believed that the same power of God would be with them as they spoke to others about Jesus's message, and that the life of Jesus would flow through them.

ABOVE: *Michelangelo's marble statue (1553) in Florence, Italy, captures the sorrow of Christ's mother as the body of her son is taken down from the Cross.*

... History of Christianity

LEFT: *Procession to celebrate Easter at a Russian Orthodox church.*

RIGHT: *William Tyndale wanted to make the scriptures available to ordinary people and he was the first to translate the New Testament directly from Greek into English. This is the title page from an edition printed in Antwerp in 1534.*

LEFT: *The procession of Our Lord of the Miracles, Lima, Peru. The Roman Catholic Church is strong throughout Latin America.*

Christianity spread quickly after the final events of Jesus's life, and it was St Paul especially who broke new ground. According to the New Testament he was a great enemy of Christians until, on the road to Damascus, a vision of Jesus stopped him in his tracks. Following his conversion to Christianity, Paul criss-crossed the eastern Mediterranean, founding churches. By the time of his death there were Christians from Spain to Palestine, and in Rome itself.

Good communications within the Roman Empire helped the new religion. However, its growth worried the imperial authorities. Christian congregations often spanned the social divide, bringing together slaves and patrician families. Christians also refused to conform to the official religion of emperor worship. Attempts were made to suppress Christianity, but this had the opposite effect. There was a saying: 'The blood of the martyrs is the seed of the Church.'

The acceptance of Christianity by Emperor Constantine in 312 swiftly changed the situation and Christianity became the official religion. But West and East in the Roman Empire began to drift apart. Initially the differences were cultural, but then became matters of teaching. The Eastern Church linked truth and mystery, while in the West the Church sought more to define and explain. The Pope claimed universal jurisdiction, which the East would not recognise. The Eastern Church became known as the Orthodox Church, the Western Church as the Catholic Church.

During the medieval period the Church began to show signs of fatigue. It had spread to almost every corner of Europe, but needed reform. Some renewal came with the new Franciscan and Dominican religious orders with their commitment to the poor, the growing towns, and universities. However, the wealth and power of the Church had opened the door to corruption. In the Reformation from 1520 onwards the Western Church split apart.

RIGHT: *Many people, particularly in Eastern Europe, paint beautiful patterns on eggs for Easter. Eggs symbolise new life and thus the resurrection of Christ.*

RIGHT: *A contemporary Nigerian crucifix. People of different countries mark the events of Christ's life in the light of their own cultures.*

Protestant Reformers like Martin Luther in Germany and John Calvin in Switzerland sought to recreate what they saw as a simpler, more biblical Christianity. Against this the Catholic Church pressed the claims of tradition and continuity, and its superiority as a global church rather than the church of one particular nation. Each side persecuted the other. By the end of the 17th century a compromise had been reached, but the reputation of Christianity was damaged, and Catholics and Protestants alike faced new challenges from sceptics.

Nevertheless the 19th century was a period of Christian expansion. The Catholic Church was already strong in Latin America. European confidence, and the creation of new colonies in Africa and elsewhere, opened up fresh horizons for Christianity. Many missionaries volunteered for this work. They were so successful that many nations and ethnic groups embraced Christianity. In fact, by the year 2000, churches in Africa and Asia were sending evangelists to Europe.

... Christian Beliefs

Christian teaching has developed over 2,000 years, but at its heart is the belief that divine life can bless and enrich human life.

Christians believe that God is Trinity, one God expressed in three Persons: Father, Son and Holy Spirit. The Son entered into human life and history by becoming Jesus of Nazareth, the Christ. He is the bridge between this world and eternity, between God and people. Christ is the human face of God, revealing God not only by his teaching but also by his example.

This communion with God in Christ is shown clearly in the Eucharist, also known as Mass or Holy Communion. This commemorates events from the night before Jesus was taken to the Cross. At supper with his disciples he blessed the bread and gave it to them saying, 'This is my body, given for you', and similarly they shared a cup of wine of which he said, 'This is my blood, shed for you.' His words had a profound impact, increased by the fact that this was a Passover meal, recalling the Jewish escape from slavery.

From its earliest days the Church remembered this last supper, and saw it as bringing new life to the people of God. Catholics believe that the bread and wine are changed and become the body and blood of Christ, bringing his real presence among believers. In the Protestant tradition, there is more emphasis on the power of the symbols to touch the heart.

LEFT: *In the first Christian centuries, the name of Christ was often symbolised by its first two letters in Greek, Chi and Rho, in monogram form. Sometimes this was imprinted on oil lamps, in remembrance of Jesus saying that he is the light of the world.*

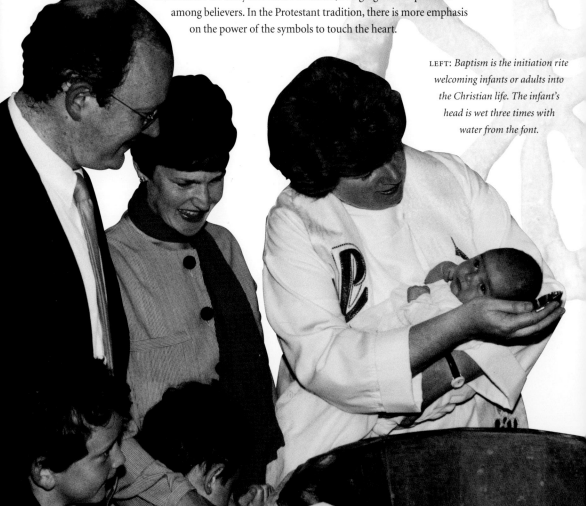

LEFT: *Baptism is the initiation rite welcoming infants or adults into the Christian life. The infant's head is wet three times with water from the font.*

Some Christians believe that new life in Christ requires a definite experience of conversion, when the believer turns aside from the life of sin and embraces a new way of living. This would be the approach of many Pentecostal, Holiness, or Bible Christian traditions. A broader tradition, however, sees conversion as weaving through ordinary life.

Christians accept the reality of sin, where people damage themselves or others by their behaviour. Christian teaching emphasises that from the perspective of God everything can be forgiven provided there is repentance and a desire to change. Christ's death on the Cross has paid the price of sin and because of this atonement no one need feel trapped.

LEFT: *Exuberant praise is typical of Pentecostal services, like this one at Kingsway International Christian Centre, Hackney, London.*

A belief in divine life through Christ is also found in the Christian understanding of baptism, or christening. Most churches baptise infants, although it can be done at any age. (Baptists will baptise only adults.) Water is poured over the head of a child three times, or the person is momentarily immersed, in the name of God – Father, Son and Holy Spirit. The new Christian can then share in the life of Christ, now and in eternity. Just as Christ has died and risen again, so too the baptised person has symbolically 'died' in the water and been raised up again with Christ.

BELOW: *Receiving communion during a Eucharist at Bath Abbey.*

Islam: The Life and Work of Muhammad

IN MUCH OF THE ARAB WORLD the dawn is greeted by a chant from the mosque proclaiming God's greatness, and Muhammad as his messenger. Muhammad was born in Mekkah in Arabia around 570. Orphaned by the age of six, he was brought up first by his grandfather and then by his uncle. Around the age of 25 he married a wealthy older widow, Khadija.

The family circle made him welcome, but his early bereavements may have made Muhammad sensitive to human suffering. Mekkah was prosperous through trading with places as far apart as India and Syria, but it was deeply divided. There were many feuds, and the tribal code of looking after one's own had collapsed. The rich neglected the poor. Muhammad found people's behaviour immoral and selfish.

ABOVE: *An 18th-century handwritten Qur'an from northern India, decorated with gold and lapis lazuli.*

Around the age of 40 he began spending long periods alone in a cave on Mount Hira, near Mekkah. The Qur'an records that during one of these times of contemplation an angel called him 'messenger of God'. Muhammad was ordered to proclaim that God was now generously prepared to teach humankind. Muhammad withdrew, shaken, but was encouraged by his wife, Khadija. About two years later similar experiences strengthened his belief that God was giving him a message for the world.

Islam

The Muslim religion is known as Islam, which derives from the Arabic for submission. The prefix M means 'a doer', hence a Muslim is one who submits to God.

Muhammad faced considerable opposition. His assertion of the one, supreme God upset Mekkahans who prospered financially from pilgrims visiting the shrines of many gods. He was also unpopular for his condemnation of immorality, and his teaching that all people were equal in the sight of God. A breakthrough came when a city 280 miles away invited him to govern them, and in 622 he migrated there with his followers. This city, now known as Medina, flourished and in 630 Mekkah itself accepted Islam. Muhammad died in Medina in 632.

The Qur'an came to Muhammad in segments over a period of 23 years. He heard sounds which would gradually form into words, a process in which his appearance and voice would change. In the Qur'an he recorded a strict moral code, the certainty of divine judgement and the importance of charity. Its words are regarded not as Muhammad's but as God directly addressing the world. It is venerated with deep respect and seen as confirming what is sound and authentic in the Jewish and Christian scriptures.

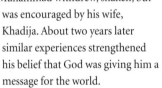
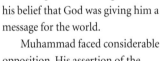

Islam came under leaders known as caliphs. The second caliph, Umar (634–44) mobilised the new faith and expanded it into Syria, Palestine, Egypt and most of Iraq. The caliphate moved to Damascus, then from 750–1258 to Baghdad, which became the centre of a flourishing international culture. By the end of the 13th century Islam stretched from Indonesia through the Middle East to North and West Africa and into Spain.

LEFT: *Muslim solidarity strengthened their armies and helped win many victories. This battle scene comes from the 16th-century* Book of Conquests *by Suleyman, which is kept in the Topkapi Museum in Istanbul.*

Sunni and Shiite

The great majority of Muslims are Sunnis, from an Arab word that means 'the traditional way'. The Shiites (from an Arabic word for 'partisan') believe that the caliphate should have passed to Muhammad's son-in-law Ali and that only a descendant of the Prophet can hold supreme office in Islam.

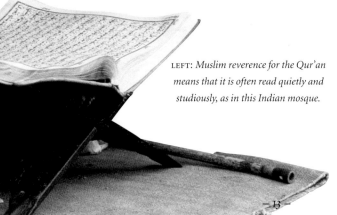

LEFT: *Muslim reverence for the Qur'an means that it is often read quietly and studiously, as in this Indian mosque.*

ABOVE: *Prayer is central to the practice of Islam – five times a day, wherever they are, Muslims stop what they are doing to pray.*

... *Faith in Action*

Muslims take pride in the clarity of their religion when it comes to guiding human behaviour. The precepts of the Qur'an are regarded as absolutely obligatory. Where necessary more precise guidance is found in the Hadith, which includes Mohammad's words and deeds, arranged by subject. From the earliest collections come the affirmation of five pillars, or essential principles, of Islam.

The first pillar is shahada, the testimony of faith: 'There is no god but God, and Muhammad is his Messenger.' Although each Muslim should say it reverently at least once in their life, in fact they do so often, as an invocation and encouragement, and with special fervour as death approaches.

The shahada also occurs within the second pillar, salat, which is observance of the required times of prayer. Each Muslim should pray five times daily: at dawn, noon, mid-afternoon, sunset, and at night. Prayers can be said at home or with others in the mosque, but men are expected to be at the mosque for communal prayer at noon on Fridays. Whether alone or not, a Muslim always faces Mekkah to pray.

Every year millions of Muslims come from all over the world on pilgrimage to Mekkah. During the pilgrimage they walk seven times around the Kaaba which is a cube-shaped stone building 15 metres (45 feet) high.

RIGHT: *Muslims offering their daily prayers must face Mekkah, and can use a special compass on a prayer mat to help them do so.*

Abraham

The patriarch Abraham is revered by Jews, Christians and Muslims. According to the Qur'an, Abraham built the Kaaba shrine and by divine instruction declared this to be a place of pilgrimage. Abraham asked God to feed the people of Mekkah and to send them a prophet, Muhammad's mission being the answer to this prayer. Other traditions add that Abraham's slave girl Hagar settled at Mekkah with their child Ismail, and that Abraham visited them there.

The third pillar is zakat, or charity. The better-off are to help the poor, ideally by giving away one-fortieth of their wealth annually.

The fourth pillar is the observance of Ramadan, the ninth month of the Islamic calendar. During this holy month Muslims fast from dawn to dusk. Ramadan, which celebrates the gift of the Qur'an, is central to Islamic spirituality. The hunger of the fast reminds all Muslims of their dependence on God, and reminds the rich of the hunger of the poor – so almsgiving is recommended in Ramadan. It is believed that abstinence from food, drink, tobacco and sex in daylight hours also heightens self-control. During Ramadan there will be many opportunities to listen to prayer and spiritual teaching.

The fifth pillar is the hajj, or pilgrimage to Mekkah. This once in a lifetime pilgrimage is obligatory for every adult male who can afford it, and for women if they can be escorted. On arrival pilgrims must change into simple, modest garments, which remove distinctions of wealth or status. During the month of pilgrimage several million Muslims may gather, bringing together people from many countries and races. Today pilgrims walk seven times around the Kaaba as part of the pilgrimage ritual. Only Muslims may enter Mekkah.

ABOVE AND LEFT: *The fasting season of Ramadan closes with the feast of Eid al-Fitr, when there is an atmosphere of rejoicing. People wear their best clothes and attend mosque, before gathering for a celebratory meal.*

...The Place of Prayer

The Muslim house of prayer is called the mosque. Like synagogues and churches, mosques vary in style according to the period of construction and the culture of the region. However, every mosque has a mihrab, or niche, indicating the direction of Mekkah. There will also usually be a minbar, or pulpit. Where women are present, a separate section is provided for them, such as a gallery.

Pictures or statues are never found in mosques, because Islam stresses that such things run the danger of idolatry. However, a mosque may be richly and beautifully decorated with intricate patterns or calligraphy in Arabic. These scripts may be excerpts from the Qur'an, or some of the traditional 99 names of God. Among these titles God is hailed as the Merciful (*Al-Rahman*), the Holy (*Al-Quddus*), the Bounteous (*Al-Karim*), and the Infinitely Patient (*As-Sabur*).

Outside the mosque there may be a minaret, or tower, from which the muezzin makes the call to prayer. There may also be running water and basins, for before prayer Muslims must wash their head, nostrils and ears, their lower arms and their feet. Shoes are left outside the mosque. At prayers in the mosque, the worshippers begin in a standing position with palms uplifted, and then bow deeply, prostrate themselves, and sit back on their heels, in time to the imam's, or leader's, praise and exultation of God. The unity of these movements, interlinking the body and the praise of God, dramatically symbolises the unity of the worshippers and the greatness of God. On Fridays the prayers may be preceded by recitation from the Qur'an and followed by a sermon.

RIGHT: *The Lotfollah Mosque in Isfahan, Iran. A typical feature of a mosque is a mihrab, or niche, indicating the direction of Mekkah.*

Sufism

The name Sufi may come from the word suf, meaning 'wool', from which garments worn by Sufis are made, or from the word safaa, meaning 'purity'. Sufis follow a mystical tradition within Islam, seeking closeness to God in a variety of ways: ascetic discipline, song, dance, and a rich literature of poetry which describes the loving union of the seeker with God. This latter especially has led to controversy within Islam.

Mosque architecture typically includes a minaret, a tower from which the call to prayer sounds forth over the surrounding area. This minaret soars above the Darwish Mosque in Amman, Jordan.

LEFT: *The whirling dance of the dervishes seeks to bring about a closer communion with God through the music and movement of the dance. This mystical movement has sometimes been controversial within Islam.*

RIGHT: *Friday prayers in an Egyptian street. Muslims sometimes fulfil the duty of prayer in public places if they cannot get to the mosque.*

One of the best-known Muslim feasts is Eid al-Fitr, the first day of the tenth month and the end of Ramadan. There is a festival atmosphere, beginning with special morning prayers and continuing with feasting and the exchange of gifts at great family gatherings. Other important feasts include Maulid al-Nabi, which commemorates the birth of Muhammad, and Eid al-Adha, the Feast of Sacrifices, linked with the story of how Abraham was provided with a ram as a sacrificial offering in place of his son. Sheep are sacrificed and the meat shared out.

LEFT: *This Muslim wedding is taking place in North London.*

Hinduism: *An Ancient Religion*

AROUND 4,500 YEARS AGO a massive movement of people began on the steppes of what is now central Russia. They moved down into the Indian sub-continent, taking with them their own religious system which merged with local traditions.

The Indo-Europeans, as they are called, passed on to their successors a religion which stressed the role of three castes: soldiers, priests and producers. They also contributed the oldest part of the Hindu scriptures, the four Vedas, composed over a period of about a thousand years. The Vedas comprise a variety of material, and include hymns to the deities, instructions for worship, and accounts of the origin of the world. They are regarded as sacred knowledge. More philosophical and mystical material is found in the Upanishads, a collection of around 250 treatises composed over many years from the late Vedic period to the modern era.

A key element in the Hindu scriptures is the concept of Brahman. Brahman is the divine reality beyond the world, unmoved and unmoving. This ultimate reality cannot be penetrated by human understanding, but is reflected through a pantheon of gods.

Vedic religion emphasised sacrifice and had its own pantheon of gods. However, around 500 BC, Vedism faded away. The stress on Brahman remained, but its main deities were supplanted by others. Three gods in particular are reflections of Brahman.

RIGHT: A statue of Shiva, surrounded by a garland of flames, dancing the dance of life and death.

Brahma is the creator of the world and is usually shown with four faces looking at the four points of the compass and holding the four Vedas in four hands. He is also shown mounted on a swan.

Vishnu is the keeper of the eternal law with a history of appearing in the world to help at crucial times, in forms known as avatar (descent). Rama and Krishna are two avatars of Vishnu and are often regarded as reflections of Brahman in their own right. Vishnu is sometimes depicted lying on a serpent with a thousand heads, floating on the surface of the cosmic waters.

Shiva is an ambivalent figure who creates and destroys, thus keeping in motion the cycle of coming into being and passing away. Shiva is often shown with a third eye in his forehead, denoting spiritual insight, or as the lord of the dance, Nataraja, surrounded by a garland of flames.

Each of these deities has its own shakti, or female counterpart.

LEFT: *A portable wooden shrine of Vishnu from Tirupati in southern India, made around 1900. Vishnu is said to appear in the world at crucial times.*

BELOW: *Cows are venerated within Hindu India, possibly because they symbolise life-giving nourishment. As part of their respect for the cow, Hindus do not eat beef.*

To the western mind, the proliferation of divine figures can seem extravagant. It is important to remember that they represent ultimate reality, in the form of Brahman, sometimes translated as the Absolute. What form of words could ever describe God adequately? None ever could. Different deities are thus representations of the divine, which in itself will always be beyond humankind. People choose their own *ishta devata*, or beloved ideal deity, to be for them the aspect of Brahman that is worshipped. Thus the number of gods is countless.

RIGHT: *The Hindu temple at Neasden in north-west London was opened in 1995. It belongs to the Swaminarayan branch of Hinduism.*

...Life and Death and Rebirth

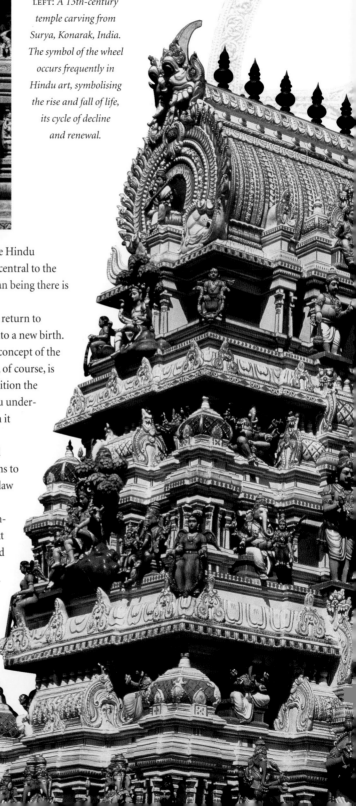

LEFT: *A 13th-century temple carving from Surya, Konarak, India. The symbol of the wheel occurs frequently in Hindu art, symbolising the rise and fall of life, its cycle of decline and renewal.*

Just as the idea of Brahman is central to the Hindu understanding of God, so the idea of atman is central to the understanding of human nature. In each human being there is the breath of the divine, atman.

This aspect of human nature is believed to return to Brahman at death, only to go out once more into a new birth. Although this has similarities to the Christian concept of the soul, there are also important differences. One, of course, is reincarnation; another is that in Christian tradition the soul is unique and personal, while in the Hindu under-standing, atman loses its individual traits when it returns to Brahman.

Hinduism describes dharma as the natural universal law whose observance enables humans to be contented and happy. Dharma is the moral law combined with spiritual discipline that guides one's life. Hinduism accepts the concept of rein-carnation. The state of an individual in the next existence is determined by his or her karma and refers to the actions undertaken by the body and the mind. To achieve good karma it is important to live life according to dharma. This involves doing what is right for the individual, the family, the class or caste and also for the universe itself.

Ten essential rules for the observance of dharma are described as patience, forgiveness, piety or self-control, honesty, sanctity, control of senses, reason, knowledge or learning, truthfulness, and absence of anger.

Death is therefore not the end, but part of a cycle of coming into being and passing away. Something of this is reflected in Hindu funeral ceremonies. The corpse is cremated on a funeral pyre, releasing the body into the atmosphere, while the remaining ashes are scattered on sacred waters. Thus the body re-enters the elements of the world, and will itself be recycled.

BELOW: *A Brahman (priest) conducting a ceremony at the Hindu temple in Southall, West London. Brahmans form one of four main castes in Hinduism: the other three being Kshatriyas (rulers and military), Vaishyas (farmers, landlords and merchants) and Sudras (peasants and workers). The untouchables have no caste and often do work considered as polluting.*

LEFT: *The elaborately carved exterior of the Bull Temple, Bangalore, India, conveys the rich panoply of gods within Hindu thought and culture.*

River Ganges

With life always depending on water, many rivers in India are sacred, especially the Ganges. Its junction with the Yamuna river near Allahabad is a pilgrimage site, as is Varanasi (Benares), where pilgrims bathe ritually. An elderly person may travel long distances to die and be cremated in Varanasi, their ashes being scattered on the Ganges. To die here is to achieve liberation from the cycle of death and rebirth, for Varanasi is regarded as the centre, not only of India, but of the cosmos.

'As the flowing rivers disappear in the sea, losing their name and their form, so a wise man, freed from name and form, goes to the divine which is greater than the great.'

ABOVE: *Pilgrims praying and bathing in the sacred River Ganges.*

FROM THE *MUNDAKA UPANISHAD*

... Temple and Home

In Hinduism the spirituality of the people is most often the path of devotion, or bhakti. This movement began in the 4th century BC and around AD 1000 developed a rich literature, notably the *Bhagavad Gita*, which itself is part of a vast epic poem, called the *Mahabharata*.

Bhakti flourished especially in Tamil-speaking areas of southern India. Here it turned away from the literary language Sanskrit to produce vernacular songs expressing the desire of ordinary people for closeness with God. Bhakti sometimes overcame divisions of caste and gender.

Bhakti is most often focused upon the god Vishnu, especially in his descent as Krishna. The best-known story of the *Bhagavad Gita* concerns Krishna's dialogue with the warrior Arjuna, who is torn apart by the fact that he must fight an opposing army containing family members, friends and mentors. Krishna's reply is that to fight is the path of duty. If Arjuna can do this with detachment – indifferent to outcome – he will find that at death he will be set free and united with the Lord, Krishna himself. At one level, this is a story of personal suffering; at another, it is about how all human effort hurries along to dissolution. In time, both victor and vanquished will disappear. To rise above the apparent divisions of this life is to find true freedom.

Most Hindu homes have a family altar, with a statue of the chosen deity. This is not an idol but an image that moves the believer to sense the divine presence. In puja – domestic worship – typical actions include lighting an oil lamp, offering flowers, incense and light, and reciting mantras.

LEFT: *The puja mark, made with red gum paste, shows that this woman has offered up prayer as part of her daily routine. Many women place this mark after worship at the shrine they keep in their home.*

BELOW: *An 18th-century Punjabi painting showing Krishna and the women of his entourage celebrating Holi, a spring festival involving fun and pranks.*

Sacred thread

As a rite of initiation a young man is given a sacred thread, made of three strands knotted together. It is worn over the left shoulder and renewed annually. For Brahman boys it marks their separateness from other castes. Traditionally it also begins the time when they study the sacred scriptures.

ABOVE: *The festival of lights, or Diwali, is a time of celebration when families come together to exchange gifts. Firecrackers are set off, houses specially decorated, and lamps are lit to celebrate the victory of good over evil and in thanksgiving for blessings.*

Temples vary greatly, but a Hindu temple might typically include a statue of the deity in a sanctuary, with a hall in front. There may be male and female sexual symbols, again symbolising the overcoming of duality.

As part of the temple ritual, priests may anoint the image of the deity, and make offerings of flowers, rice and sweets. As the ceremony closes the priest makes a circular motion with lamps in front of the image, taking the lamps to the worshippers who cup their hands over the flame and touch their faces, bringing the light and warmth of the deity to themselves. They leave with a red spot or white ash mark on their forehead to show that they have fulfilled the ritual.

ABOVE: *Hindu sacred writings contain many epic stories of battle, such as the scenes that decorate the entrance arch of this temple in Vishnapur, India.*

Buddhism: *The Enlightened One*

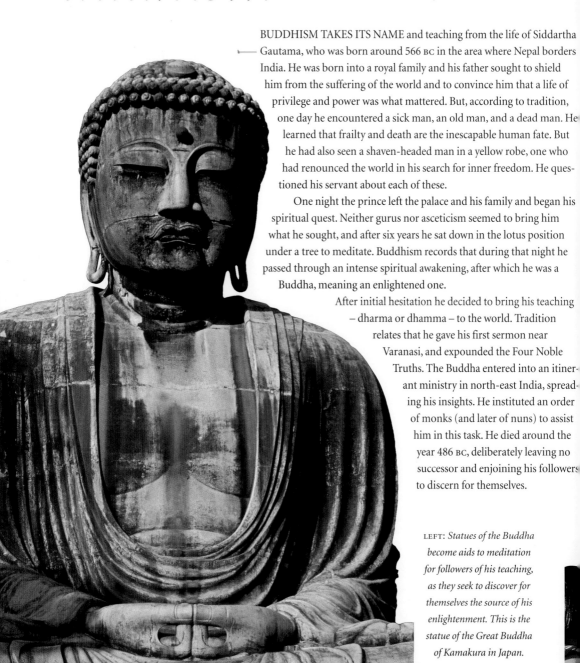

BUDDHISM TAKES ITS NAME and teaching from the life of Siddartha Gautama, who was born around 566 BC in the area where Nepal borders India. He was born into a royal family and his father sought to shield him from the suffering of the world and to convince him that a life of privilege and power was what mattered. But, according to tradition, one day he encountered a sick man, an old man, and a dead man. He learned that frailty and death are the inescapable human fate. But he had also seen a shaven-headed man in a yellow robe, one who had renounced the world in his search for inner freedom. He questioned his servant about each of these.

One night the prince left the palace and his family and began his spiritual quest. Neither gurus nor asceticism seemed to bring him what he sought, and after six years he sat down in the lotus position under a tree to meditate. Buddhism records that during that night he passed through an intense spiritual awakening, after which he was a Buddha, meaning an enlightened one.

After initial hesitation he decided to bring his teaching – dharma or dhamma – to the world. Tradition relates that he gave his first sermon near Varanasi, and expounded the Four Noble Truths. The Buddha entered into an itinerant ministry in north-east India, spreading his insights. He instituted an order of monks (and later of nuns) to assist him in this task. He died around the year 486 BC, deliberately leaving no successor and enjoining his followers to discern for themselves.

LEFT: *Statues of the Buddha become aids to meditation for followers of his teaching, as they seek to discover for themselves the source of his enlightenment. This is the statue of the Great Buddha of Kamakura in Japan.*

A stupa is a shrine containing relics of the Buddha or his disciples. This dome-shaped stupa in Nepal follows the architectural style of the oldest stupas.

The Four Noble Truths

First, that life is suffering (dukkha). By this Buddhism means more than hardship. It means, rather, that to accept life is to accept reality, with its uncertainty, transience and vulnerability.

Second, that an endless chain of death and rebirth is taking place, caused by pervasive human desire. Buddhism differs from other major religions in having no doctrine of a personal soul – or for that matter of a divine universal reality. What is reborn is more like an energy, the ongoing consequences of choices made during one's life.

Third, that suffering will only cease when craving is removed. This will in turn allow nirvana, a state of inner freedom and peace. Being reborn ceases also.

Fourth, that the way to nirvana is found by embracing the Noble Eightfold Path (see page 26), which is the core of Buddhist spirituality.

Subsequently differing traditions arose. Mahayana Buddhism groups together diverse traditions found in Nepal, Tibet, China, Mongolia, Japan and Vietnam. This tradition has tended to elevate the Buddha to a semi-divine status from which he still influences the world. Mahayana teaches that a person can become a Bodhisattva, or compassionate being, dedicated to helping others on their path to nirvana. Theravada Buddhism is found in Sri Lanka, Myanmar, Thailand, Laos and Cambodia. It draws much of it spiritual vitality from monastic orders and sees the Buddha as an example rather than as a saviour. Theravada stresses the practice of meditation.

RIGHT: *Shwe Dagon Pagoda is an ancient Buddhist temple in Rangoon, Myanmar (formerly Burma). It stands 100 metres (325 feet) high and is covered in gold leaf. About 87 per cent of the people of Myanmar are Theravada Buddhists.*

BELOW: *Women lighting sticks of incense at a Buddhist shrine in Japan.*

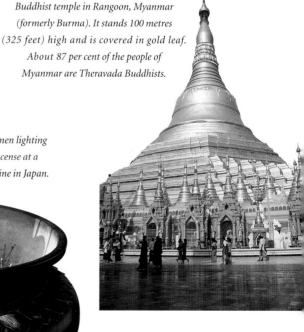

... Faith and Practice

At the heart of Buddhist faith is the Noble Eightfold Path, which is traditionally seen as the fourth of the noble truths preached by the Buddha. It is a way of self-discipline. Right mindfulness, for example, can take the form of a walking meditation in which there is a single-minded concentration on each component of taking a step, the intention being to develop a similar discipline when it comes to thoughts and emotions.

But Buddhism is found in a wide range of cultures and reflects elements of these in its spirituality. From Tibet, for example, has come Tantric Buddhism, which uses tools such as mantras and mandalas. A mantra is a chant which may be in words which only the guru may know the meaning of, until it is divulged. A mandala is a diagram, sometimes of intricate design, symbolising cosmic or spiritual powers. Different again is Zen Buddhism, which originated in China as Ch'an and developed in Japan. Zen seeks to break down conventional, ingrained patterns of thinking and understanding so that a new insight may emerge. To this end meditation is central, but Zen masters also challenge their disciples through irony, conundrums, paradoxes and iconoclasm.

LEFT: *A mandala is a circular diagram used in Buddhist ritual and meditation. It can represent the forces at work in the world and how these can be overcome by those who find the right path. A mandala may be painted on paper or cloth, traced on the ground with coloured sands, or built in stone.*

The Noble Eightfold Path

RIGHT UNDERSTANDING
Understanding the Four Noble Truths and seeing how life experience verifies them.

RIGHT THOUGHT
Commitment and persistence in following the path.

RIGHT SPEECH
To speak truthfully and without malice.

RIGHT ACTION
Living with integrity, conforming to the Five Precepts: do not kill, do not steal, do not lie, live in a sexually disciplined way, avoid intoxicants.

RIGHT LIVELIHOOD
Finding a constructive and harmless occupation.

RIGHT EFFORT
Taking control of one's thoughts in a balanced and disciplined way.

RIGHT MINDFULNESS
Scrutiny of one's mental and emotional processes so that a healthy self-awareness is reached, allowing wisdom to arise.

RIGHT CONCENTRATION
This, combined with the other factors in the Path, leads to a deep transformation.

Sangha, or monastic life, dates back to the time of the Buddha himself. After a period of training a novice becomes a bhikku (monk) or bhikkuni (nun). Monks may wear an orange or yellow robe, and depend on alms for their welfare. They follow an ancient monastic rule with many precepts, aimed at shaping the life of the community so that it mirrors Buddhist ideals to the world. All aim at growth in wisdom and understanding. To become a Buddhist monk or nun need not be a lifetime commitment: those seeking enlightenment may enter monastic life for a limited period.

ABOVE: *The tranquillity of Zen gardens is not an end in itself, but intended to encourage meditation which leads the seeker beyond conventional understanding to an experience of utter reality itself.*

Buddhist scriptures

Buddhist teaching is enshrined in sayings ascribed to the Buddha, and transmitted in Theravada Buddhism by the Pali Canon. This collection of texts is written in Pali, an ancient language akin to Sanskrit and written down around the 1st century BC.

ABOVE AND LEFT: *Buddhist monks clad in the traditional saffron robes of one seeking enlightenment. The bowls will be used as they go round the streets begging for alms.*

Sikhism: Followers of the Path

THE WORD SIKH MEANS DISCIPLE, a follower of the path as shown by the Gurus of the religion. The first Guru, and founder of Sikhism, was Guru Nanak (1469–1539) who was born in north-west India, in what is now Pakistan.

For centuries there had been rivalry between the differing Hindu and Muslim traditions in India. One day, Guru Nanak entered into a mystical experience while bathing in a river. After three days he announced that he had been commissioned to bring a new message to the world. The message instructed that what mattered in life was to follow God's path, and that ultimately there was no Hindu and no Muslim.

Sikhs therefore regard their own origin as divine. God is seen as beyond human conceiving and without form. Sikhism rejects the Hindu concept of God appearing as avatar in an incarnation or descent on earth. Sikhism also does away with caste, and believes that reincarnation depends on a person's karma.

Guru Nanak together with a Muslim minstrel, Mardana, travelled widely to spread this message. Many of their hymns became an important element in Sikh worship. Other Gurus succeeded Guru Nanak. Guru Arjun compiled the Adi Granth, the Sikh scriptures. They were given the title Guru Granth Sahib after Guru Gobind Singh decided that no other mortal would succeed him as Guru. The holy scriptures are treated with respect and honour, as a living Guru.

RIGHT: *The Guru's Bridge and the Golden Temple of Amritsar, in the Punjab, north-west India. The temple with its gilded roofs was built in the 18th century and is Sikhism's holiest shrine.*

The sacred writings are mostly inspired poems and hymns that are the fruits of the meditation of the Gurus. The scriptures emphasise purity of motivation and union with the All Mighty. In the Sikh Gurdwara, or temple, the holy scriptures are the only object for veneration and are placed on a raised throne under a canopy. There are priests at the Gurdwara but any member of the community, man, woman or child, can read at services. On many special occasions the Guru Granth is read continuously from start to finish, which takes around 48 hours. All Sikh temples have communal kitchens and dining halls where meals are served to all who come, without discrimination. So those who come to the Gurdwara first serve others, then themselves eat, before paying their respects to Guru Granth Sahib.

A key moment in the evolution of Sikhism came when Guru Gobind Singh created an order known as the Khalsa, or pure ones. Those joining it become full members of the Sikh religion and must abstain from halal meat, tobacco, cutting of hair and adultery. They must also keep the five K's with them at all times: kes (uncut hair, often covered by a turban); kangha (wooden comb); kara (bangle); kachera (knee-length breeches); and kirpan (sword). All Khalsa are given the same name – Singh (lion) for men, Kaur (princess) for women.

BELOW: *The wedding of two Sikhs in Leeds. During the marriage ceremony the bride and groom walk around the book of Guru Granth Sahib four times to show how important it will be in their life together.*